What Is Dilig

Write in the circles the appropriate number for each definition.

1 Diligence is paying close attention to the tiniest detail.

2 Being diligent is doing the little steps well, to make the end product good.

3 Diligence is especially important when trying to get good grades.

4 Diligence is being faithful with something, a little each day to get good at it.

5 Diligence is to make the best use of your time.

A Little Play

Write your name on the dotted line below, then see how many small words you can make from the sentence.

.... is diligent!

....

....

....

....

....

Number these jobs from 1 to 12, in the order you prefer to do them.

Make bed ☐   Scrub sink ☐   Vacuuming ☐

Fold laundry ☐   Take out trash ☐   Brush teeth ☐

Dishes ☐   Dusting ☐   Put toys away ☐

Clean toilet ☐   Sweeping ☐   Water plants ☐

Diligence is to do a good job, and to continue something till it's done.
Be organized and concentrate, and do each thing one by one.

Give it Your Best

Diligence grows from responsibility. So if responsibility is knowing your job and doing it, then diligence is doing your best at your job.

A job diligently done is a job well-done.

Draw how the jobs might get done with and without diligence. See examples below.

WITH DILIGENCE

gardening

setting the table

putting toys away

washing the car

WITHOUT DILIGENCE

doing homework

folding clothes

wiping the table

building a house

Little Things

Being diligent and faithful with little things is very important because without the little things there wouldn't be any big things. If we are faithful with the little things we have, then God can bless us with bigger things.

Write on the rocks what BIG THINGS these little tiny things might turn into, and then draw a line to match each one.

GRAINS OF SAND

DROPS OF WATER

LITTLE SEEDS

TINY LETTERS

Snakes and Ladders

Invite a friend, parent or sibling to play this fun game with you.
You will need: a die, and some buttons or Lego pieces for markers.

First player rolls the die and places his marker on the number indicated. Read and follow the instructions on the game board. Remember that when you land on a ladder, you climb up. But when you land on a snake, you slide down. The winner is the first one to reach the END!

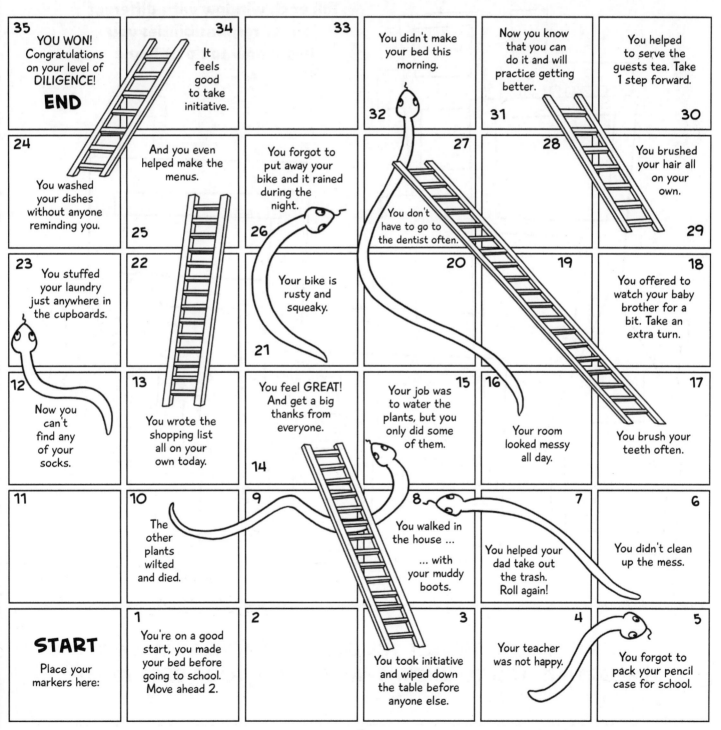

35 YOU WON! Congratulations on your level of DILIGENCE! **END**

34 It feels good to take initiative.

33

32 You didn't make your bed this morning.

31 Now you know that you can do it and will practice getting better.

30 You helped to serve the guests tea. Take 1 step forward.

24 You washed your dishes without anyone reminding you.

And you even helped make the menus. **25**

26 You forgot to put away your bike and it rained during the night.

27 You don't have to go to the dentist often.

28

You brushed your hair all on your own. **29**

23 You stuffed your laundry just anywhere in the cupboards.

22

Your bike is rusty and squeaky. **21**

20

19

18 You offered to watch your baby brother for a bit. Take an extra turn.

12 Now you can't find any of your socks.

13 You wrote the shopping list all on your own today.

You feel GREAT! And get a big thanks from everyone. **14**

15 Your job was to water the plants, but you only did some of them.

16 Your room looked messy all day.

17 You brush your teeth often.

11

10 The other plants wilted and died.

9

8 You walked in the house ... ... with your muddy boots.

You helped your dad take out the trash. Roll again!

7

6 You didn't clean up the mess.

START Place your markers here:

1 You're on a good start, you made your bed before going to school. Move ahead 2.

2

3 You took initiative and wiped down the table before anyone else.

4 Your teacher was not happy.

5 You forgot to pack your pencil case for school.

In the House

How does it feel to know how to do different jobs and things around the house?

. . . .

. . . .

Fill each window with different jobs or responsibilities you know how to do at home.

IT'S NOT HOW PERFECT THE JOB GETS DONE THAT'S SO IMPORTANT, IT'S TO KNOW THAT YOU DID YOUR BEST AT IT!

Above All ...

It's important to learn to get things done right, to be faithful and diligent in all the little details. But above all things, we want to focus on the heart, doing these things out of love for God and others. Join the numbered dots to finish the picture.

Everything we do can be an act of worship to God. Colossians 3:23

In the end, we won't only learn diligence, but we will also learn godliness.

The Diligent ...

What the Bible has to say about diligent people ...

Doodle around the Scripture verses. What comes to mind as you read them?

Diligent people ...

WILL BECOME LEADERS
The hand of the diligent will rule. (Proverbs 12:24)

WILL OBTAIN WEALTH AND PROSPER
The soul of the diligent shall be made rich. (Proverbs 13:4)

HAVE A DEFINITE PURPOSE AND PLAN
Be diligent to make sure you're doing what you've been called to do, for if you do these things you will not fall. (2 Peter 1:10)

WORK EVEN WHEN IT IS INCONVENIENT
Be strong and do not let your hands be weak, for your work shall be rewarded! (2 Chronicles 15:7)

WILL BE SUCCESSFUL
Do you see a man who is diligent in his work? He will serve kings and not just ordinary people.

(Proverbs 22:29)

The Lazy ...

What the Bible has to say about lazy people ...

Doodle around the Scripture verses. What comes to mind as you read them?

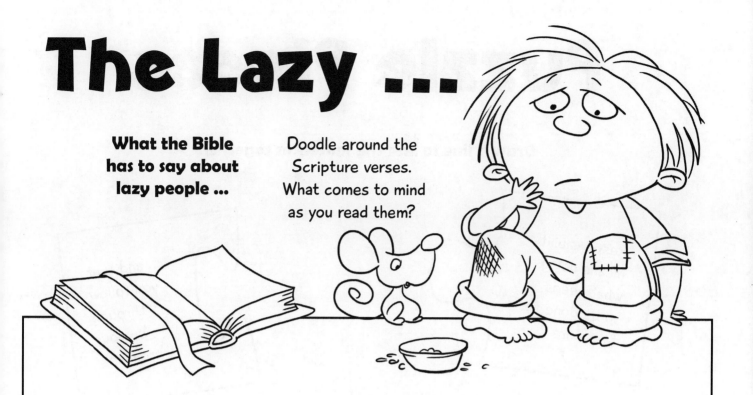

Lazy people ...

HAVE TROUBLE STARTING THEIR WORK

Working hard pays off. But if all you do is talk, you will be poor. (Proverbs 14:23)

HAVE TROUBLE FINISHING THEIR WORK

A lazy man goes hunting and catches prey,
but then doesn't even cook the meal after. (Proverbs 12:27)

The lazy man doesn't feel like plowing his field in autumn.
So at harvest time, there is nothing left for him to eat. (Proverbs 20:4)

ONLY WANT TO PLAY

Whoever only wants to play and have fun will end up being poor. (Proverbs 21:17)

DON'T GET ANYTHING

People who refuse to work, want and need things but get nothing. (Proverbs 13:4)

Those who are unwilling to work don't get to eat. (2 Thessalonians 3:10)

Puzzle Pieces

Draw a line to link the sentences together.

Responsibility means doing what needs to be done to take care ...

... and that you follow through on your promises.

Being responsible means that others can rely on you ...

... of yourself, your family, your friends, and the greater community.

Sometimes acting responsibly might involve doing something difficult ...

... no to something that could be wrong for you to do.

Responsibility can ask for moral strength, like saying ...

... like studying for a test or giving up social plans in favor of helping the family.

Start Small

If learning diligence and responsibility is a new thing for you, just start small and simple. Begin by doing one thing all on your own, without your parents having to remind you about it. You will see that it will be easier to do other things from then on. Here is a list of some of the main responsibilities that can get done in your home:

SELF SKILLS
- GET DRESSED
- GET UP ON MY OWN
- TAKE A SHOWER OR BATH
- MAKE BREAKFAST
- ORGANIZE HOMEWORK
- MAKE BED
- WASH HAIR
- DRY AND BRUSH HAIR
- PACK BACKPACK
- ORGANIZE MY TIME
- BRUSH TEETH
- REMEMBER SPORTS GEAR
- CLEAN MY ROOM

LIFE SKILLS
- SET THE TABLE
- DO LAUNDRY
- VACUUM FLOOR
- LEARN TO COOK
- UNLOAD DISHWASHER
- STACK WOOD
- CLEAN BATHROOM
- CREATE MENUS
- CLEAN KITCHEN
- PREPARE LUNCH
- MAKE SHOPPING LIST
- HELP WITH SHOPPING
- ANSWER PHONE

LIFE LESSONS
- ORGANIZATION
- TIME MANAGEMENT
- FOLLOW THROUGH
- TAKE RESPONSIBILITY
- CREATE ROUTINES
- IDENTIFY PERSONAL PREFERENCES (EXAMPLE: BATH OR SHOWER)

Mark the things that you know how to do well in RED, the things you still need more practice with in YELLOW and the things that you want to learn in BLUE.

Illustrate a
Bible Story

Read the Bible story on diligence
and have fun illustrating it.

(Genesis 1)

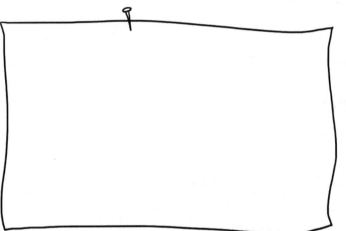

IN THE VERY BEGINNING, THERE WAS
ABSOLUTELY NOTHING. NO SHINING
SUN, NO CUDDLY ANIMALS, NO SWEET
SMELLING FLOWERS, AND NOT EVEN
PEOPLE LIKE YOU AND ME.

SO GOD DECIDED TO MAKE THE WORLD
AND FILL IT WITH THE MOST BEAUTIFUL
PLANTS, THE MOST INTERESTING
CREATURES AND THE MOST AMAZING
PEOPLE.

HE ADDED PLENTY OF OTHER THINGS TOO,
LIKE SPLASHING WATER, FLYING BIRDS,
PUFFY CLOUDS AND TWINKLING STARS.

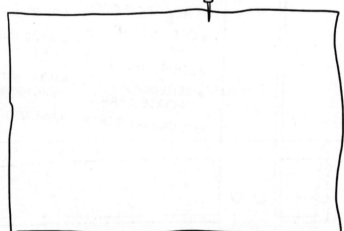

WHEN GOD FINISHED, HE SAW THAT
IT TURNED OUT VERY GOOD. HE WAS
PLEASED WITH HIS WORK AND KNEW THAT
WE WOULD ENJOY IT TOO.

Story

Application

I'M ALLIE!
I'M READY TO HELP
YOU APPLY GOD'S
WORD TO YOUR
OWN LIFE STORY.

When we look at God's **CREATION**, from the
HUGE ocean to the tiniest ant, it **SHOWS** us how God took
TIME and extra **CARE** to make it very **GOOD**. He worked until it was
just **PERFECT** and He didn't stop until it was **FINISHED**. He paid
ATTENTION to every detail and when it was all done, He took
the time to rest and **RELAX** and **ENJOY** His handiwork.

Find the bolded words from the paragraph above in this word search.

```
T M H Y W J O T P W E P G V T
Z E A M Y V X C B W W T I M E
G W M G O O D I R D P G Y W U
A D W P R B N L O R T N O C R
H R X U T S K G F L V W C K F
U W P E R F E C T I D O R O A
G C B E S Y N S C S J Z E B T
E G E K X S Z G D T X K A F T
A D N J F I N I S H E D T F E
X A J O P G M R N N A W I S N
B J O A N Q M A F E N L O Z T
C B Y R Y E P U G D E V N T I
A C I G B S H O W S R D R V O
R K T V I W O D I H K Q Y D N
E M W T R R R E L A X U N K J T
```

13

Find Your Way

Bobby is trying to find all the things that he can clean in a bubbly sort of way. Draw them in the giant bubbles and then help him make his way to each one.

Rewards/Consequences

The way we take care of doing certain jobs can either bring us rewards and blessings or consequences.

Write some possible positive or negative consequences to these examples:

Forgot to water the plants _____

Let the food boil over _____

Set a timer for the cookies in the oven _____

Followed instructions for building a house _____

Left room a mess _____

Fed the pet _____

Finished homework _____

Forgot to wash dirty laundry _____

Swept up the dirt behind the bed _____

Left dirty dishes out _____

Brushed teeth after each meal _____

Animal Kingdom

GOD GIVES US EXAMPLES OF DILIGENCE AND HARD WORK
THROUGH SOME OF THE ANIMALS THAT HE HAS MADE.

Read the animal clues.

Then draw a line to the correct animal.

1. He soars high to see things from a distance in order to spot his prey. He has good vision. We need vision before starting a job, to see what we want done.

2. He works hard building his home from huge trees. When his home gets damaged, he starts again, right back to work and never quits.

3. From a very young age, he learns quickly how to find berries, roots and nuts. He also learns how to catch fish, hunt and keep himself from danger. He has to practice for a long time before he catches his first fish.

4. Despite his tiny size, his little spirit is immensely strong with a will to get things done. He spends most of his time gathering food and taking care of his nest. When a job is too hard for him to do alone, he will get help, and then they will work together to get the job done.

5. After the mother lays an egg, the father keeps it safe and warm under a thick fold of his skin for about 54 days. No matter how cold or hungry he gets, he doesn't leave the egg until it finally hatches. It takes a lot of patience and diligence not to stop until the egg is ready.

6. His work shows effort and diligence. He works so hard and rarely takes a break. He lives to work and he makes quality tasty work.

What Others Do

Read some ideas of what other kids do in their homes, to practice diligence.
Fill in the blanks with the words from the box.

DILIGENCE	WEEK
CLOCK	JOBS
DESSERT	AROUND
CLEAN	CARE

WE SET OUR _ _ _ _ _ FOR 10-15 MINUTES EACH DAY TO TIDY UP SOMETHING AROUND THE HOME.

UNDER OUR PLATE OF SPECIAL _ _ _ _ _ _ _ ONCE A _ _ _ _, THERE IS A LIST OF JOBS THAT WE GET TO HELP WITH FOR THE WEEK.

OUR FAMILY READS PROVERBS EACH DAY. IT TALKS A LOT ABOUT _ _ _ _ _ _ _ _ _.

IN MY HOME, EACH PERSON IS RESPONSIBLE FOR KEEPING A DIFFERENT AREA OF THE HOUSE _ _ _ _ _.

EACH WEEK WE DECIDE WHICH _ _ _ _ WE WOULD LIKE TO HELP WITH AT HOME.

WHEN A CERTAIN SONG PLAYS, WE KNOW THAT IT'S TIME TO "CLEAN-UP" _ _ _ _ _ _ THE HOUSE.

I JUST GOT A PET, SO I CAN PRACTICE DILIGENCE BY TAKING _ _ _ _ OF IT.

Diddly DOOD Messy Mess!

DIDDLY COMES HOME FROM SCHOOL, DUMPS HER BAG ON THE FLOOR, TAKES OUT HER BOOKS AND THINGS AND LEAVES THEM ON THE DESK.

I'M HUNGRY FOR A SNACK! HEY, THIS BANANA LOOKS GOOD AND TASTES GOOD TOO!

I HAVEN'T SEEN MY DOLLIES ALL DAY. I NEED SOME MOMMY-BABY TIME!

DIDDLY FEELS LIKE CHANGING HER CLOTHES. SHE HAS A HARD TIME DECIDING WHAT TO WEAR. "I HAVE SO MANY TO CHOOSE FROM," SHE SAYS.

DINNER TIME, KIDS!

ALREADY? OKAY, BUT I JUST NEED TO FINISH DOING MY HAIR.

BEING DILIGENT IS TO PUT THINGS AWAY IN THEIR PLACE.

OH, I KNOW HOW TO BE DILIGENT. BUT ... LOOKS LIKE I LEFT OUT MY BOOKS, MY SCHOOLBAG, MY CLOTHES, MY TOYS, AND UGH ... EVEN MY BANANA PEEL.

YIKES! EVERYWHERE I LOOK IT'S A MESS. BUT I REALLY DON'T FEEL LIKE CLEANING IT ALL UP. AFTER ALL, IT'S DINNER TIME AND I'M WAY TOO HUNGRY TO WORK NOW.

What Would You Do?

- What should Diddly do? What would YOU do?

- What is something that you do that shows diligence?

- Can you think of a practical idea to make it easier for you to be diligent?

Draw what you think the ending of the story could turn out to be:

Play and Do

Try out these simple exercises or games to help you practice diligence.

1 Create coupons for special tasks you can do at home to help your family. Then see the positive reactions from you and your family.

2 Make yourself a daily checklist of all the things you would like to get done each day. Track your results to see how well you do after a week. See how great you feel about it.

1 make my bed
2 do my dishes
3 empty the dishwasher
4 put laundry in basket
5 feed the dog
6 take out the trash

3 Make yourself a weekly checklist. Once you reach your goal, treat yourself to a little reward, like watching your favorite TV series, a special snack, extra time with your parents, etc.

4 Next time you see your friends, take a poll. List all the jobs that you do at home to help your family. Then see how many other kids also do that in their homes or what other things they know how to do to practice diligence. What kind of results did you get?

Watch Your Clock

Here's an activity you could try out to help you be diligent with time.
Create your own paper clocks that show your scheduled times for different tasks, such as getting up, eating breakfast, dressing, leaving for school, etc. Then you can place them next to your real clock at home, to remind you of when to do things. Be as creative as you can, coming up with helpful shapes to remind you of what needs to be done at certain times.

MY CLOCK TELLS ME THAT IT'S TIME TO GET DRESSED, SO I'D BETTER GET GOING!

NO WONDER I WAS FEELING HUNGRY. MY CLOCK TELLS ME IT'S SNACK TIME!

THAT SOUND I HEAR ... I KNOW, I KNOW. IT'S REMINDING ME TO BRUSH MY TEETH!

Prayer Time

Prayer is always the best place to start when you're learning any new habit, routine or responsibility.

Here are some simple steps to your prayer time:

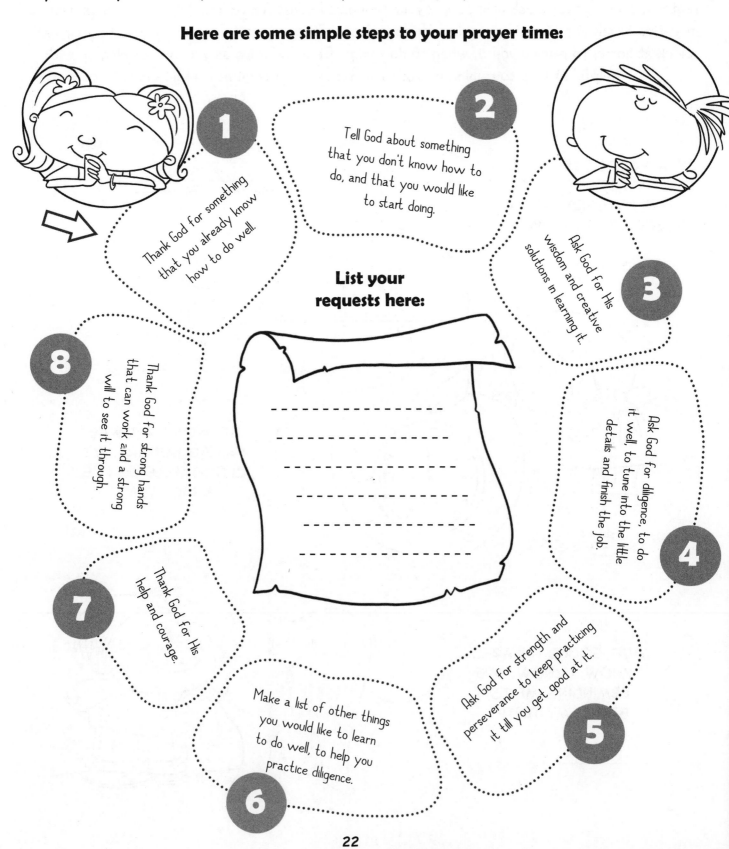

1 Thank God for something that you already know how to do well.

2 Tell God about something that you don't know how to do, and that you would like to start doing.

3 Ask God for His wisdom and creative solutions in learning it.

4 Ask God for diligence, to do it well, to tune into the little details and finish the job.

5 Ask God for strength and perseverance to keep practicing it till you get good at it.

6 Make a list of other things you would like to learn to do well, to help you practice diligence.

7 Thank God for His help and courage.

8 Thank God for strong hands that can work and a strong will to see it through.

List your requests here:

I Take Responsibility

It helps to have some sort of plan to follow when you want to start a new habit or make progress in a certain area. Since we're on the topic of diligence and responsibility, how about listing some ways that you could do better with that?

Start with number 1 and fill in the blanks till the end goal!

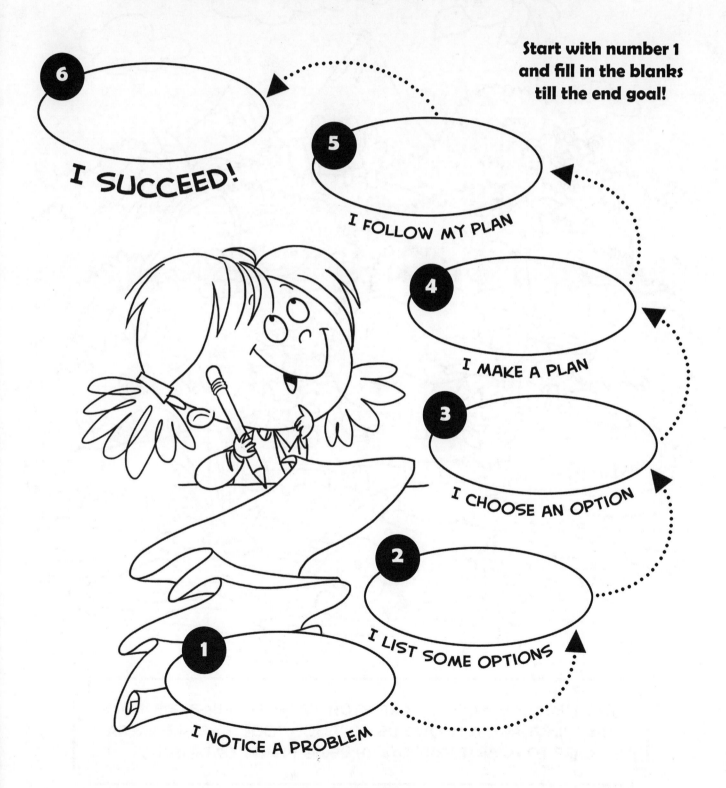

6

I SUCCEED!

5 I FOLLOW MY PLAN

4 I MAKE A PLAN

3 I CHOOSE AN OPTION

2 I LIST SOME OPTIONS

1 I NOTICE A PROBLEM

Coloring Page

Color the Bible picture.

WHEN WE LOOK AT GOD'S CREATION, FROM THE HUGE OCEAN TO THE TINIEST ANT, IT SHOWS US HOW GOD TOOK TIME AND EXTRA CARE TO MAKE IT VERY GOOD, USING PLENTY OF DILIGENCE.

Answer Sheet

What Is Diligence? - Page 1

Little Things - Page 4

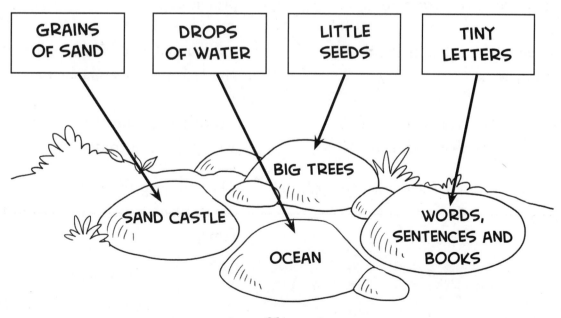

Above All ... - Page 7

Puzzle Pieces - Page 10

Responsibility means doing what needs to be done to take care ...

... and that you follow through on your promises.

Being responsible means that others can rely on you ...

... of yourself, your family, your friends and the greater community.

Sometimes acting responsibly might involve doing something difficult ...

... no to something that could be wrong for you to do.

Responsibility can ask for moral strength, like saying ...

... like studying for a test or giving up social plans in favor of helping the family.

Story Application - Page 13

```
T M H Y W J O T P W E P G V T
Z E A M Y V X C B W W T I M E
G W M G O O D I R D P G Y W U
A D W P R B N L O R T N O C R
H R X U T S K G F L V W C K F
U W P E R F E C T I D O R O A
G C B E S Y N S C S J Z E B T
E G E K X S Z G D T X K A F T
A D N J F I N I S H E D T F E
X A J O P G M R N N A W I S N
B J O A N Q M A F E N L O Z T
C B Y R Y E P U G D E V N T I
A C I G B S H O W S R D R V O
R K T V I W O D I H K Q Y D N
E M W T R R E L A X U N K J T
```

Find Your Way - Page 14

27

Animal Kingdom - Page 16

1. Eagle

4. Ant

6. Bee

5. Penguin

2. Beaver

3. Bear

What Others Do - Page 17

- We set our **clock** for 10-15 minutes each day to tidy up something around the home.
- Under our plate of special **dessert** once a **week**, there is a list of jobs that we get to help with for the week.
- Our family reads Proverbs every day, it talks a lot about **diligence**.
- In my home, each person is responsible for keeping a different area of the house **clean**.
- Each week we decide which **jobs** we would like to help with at home.
- When a certain song plays, we know that it's time to "clean-up" **around** the house.
- I just got a pet so I can practice diligence by taking **care** of it.